MINISTERING IN VIEW OF JUDGMENT DAY
TWO SERMONS

Lemuel Haynes

GLH Publishing
LOUISVILLE, KY

Sourced from:
Sketches of the Life and Character of Rev. Lemuel Haynes, by Timothy Cooley, New York: Harper & Brothers, 1837.
The Character and Work of a Spiritual Watchman Described, Litchfield, Connecticut: Printed by Collier and Buel, 1792.

GLH Publishing Reprint, 2021

ISBN:
Paperback 978-1-64863-036-1
Epub 978-1-64863-052-1

For information on new releases, weekly deals, and free ebooks visit
www.GLHpublishing.com

CONTENTS

Sermon I.

The Character and Work of a Spiritual Watchman
Described 1

Sermon II.

The Important concerns of Ministers, and the
People of their Charge, at the Day of Judgment 17

Sermon I.

THE CHARACTER AND WORK OF A SPIRITUAL WATCHMAN DESCRIBED

A SERMON DELIVERED AT HINESBURGH
FEBRUARY 13, 1791
AT THE ORDINATION OF THE REV. REUBEN PARMERLEE

For they watch over your souls as they that must give account.
Hebrews xiii. 17.

Nothing is more evident, than that men are prejudiced against the gospel. It is from this source that those who are for the defense of it meet with so much contempt. It is true, they are frail, sinful dust and ashes in common with other men; yet on account of the important embassy with which they are entrusted, it is agreeable to the unerring dictates of inspiration to esteem them very highly in love for their work's sake. 1 Thess. v. 13.

To illustrate this sentiment was the design of the Apostle of this verse, "Obey them that have the rule over you, and submit yourself." He was far from inculcating anything that might seem to confront what the Apostle Peter has enjoined, 1 Pet. v. 3. Neither as being lords over God's heritage. The word signifies to lead, guide or direct.

Our text contains an important motive to excite to attention and respect that is due to the ministers of Christ on account of their relation to him; and that is the aspect of their work has to Judgment Day: For they watch for your souls, as they that must quickly give account. They are amenable to their great Lord and Master for every sermon they preach, and must give an account of the reception they and their work meet with among their hearers.

Under the influence of such a thought, let us take notice to a few things, supposed by the work, assigned to ministers in the text.—Say something with respect to their character—Whence it appears that they must give account.—When they must be said to be properly influenced by such considerations.

I. There are several ideas suggested by the work assigned to gospel ministers in the text: which is, to *watch for souls*. This supposes,

1. That the goal is of vast importance, else why so much attention paid to it, as to have a guard to inspect it? All those injunctions which we find interspersed through the sacred pages to watchmen to be faithful are so many evidences of the worth of men's souls. What renders them so valuable is the important relation they stand in to their Maker. The perfections of the Deity are more illustrated in the redemption of fallen men, than they would have been in the salvation of apostate angels; else why were the latter passed by, while God chose the former as the objects of his attention? God has from eternity appointed a proper number for the display of his mercy and justice; means are necessary to fit for the Master's use; so that the soul in this view is of infinite importance.

2. Watchmen over the souls of men implies that they are prone to neglect them or to be inattentive to their souls. When one is set to inspect or watch over another it supposes some kind of incapacity that he is under to take care of himself. The Scripture represents mankind by nature as *fools, madmen*, and being in a state of *darkness*, &c.

Men in general are very sagacious with respect to temporal affairs, and display much natural wit and ingenuity and contriving and accomplishing evil designs; but to do good, they have no knowledge. Jer. iv. 22. This is an evidence that their inability to foresee danger and provide against it is that the moral kind. Were there a disposition in mankind corresponding to their natural powers to secure the eternal interest of their souls and the way God has prescribed, watchmen would be in great measure useless.

3. The work and office of gospel ministers suggests the idea of enemies invading; that there is a controversy subsisting in a danger approaching. When soldiers are called fourth and sentinels stand up on the wall it denotes war. The souls of men are environed with ten thousand enemies that are seeking their ruin. Earth and hell are combined to destroy. How many already have fell victims to their ferocity! The infernal powers are daily dragging away their prey to the prison of hell. Men have rebelled against God and have made him their enemy; yea, all creatures and all events are working the eternal misery of the finally impenitent sinner.

4. We are taught in the text and elsewhere, that the work of a gospel minister is not with the temporal, but the spiritual concerns of men: They watch for *souls*. Their conversation is not to be about worldly affairs, but things that relate to Christ's kingdom, which involves the everlasting concerns of mens souls. When a minister's affections are upon this world, his visits among his people will be barren; he will inquire about

the outward circumstances of his flock; and perhaps, from pecuniary motives, rejoice at such prosperity. But as though that was of greatest concern, he will have nothing to say with respect to the health and prosperity of their souls; have no joys or sorrows, to express, on account of the fruitful or more lifeless state of the inward man.

II. Let us say something with respect to the character of the spiritual watchman.

Natural endowments embellished with a good education are qualifications obviously requisite for an evangelical minister; that it is needless that we insist upon them at the same time and that the interest of religion has and still continues greatly to suffer for the want them is equally notorious.

In the early ages of Christianity, men were miraculously qualified and called into the work of gospel ministry; but we are far from believing that this is the present mode by which ordinary ministers are introduced.

1. It is necessary that those who engage in this work, love the cause in which they profess to be embarked; that the love of Christ be shed abroad in the heart: Hence our blessed Lord, by those repeated interrogations to Simon whether he loved him, has set before us the importance of this qualification in a spiritual shepherd. The sad consequences of admitting those into the army who are in heart enemies of the commonwealth have often taught men to be careful in this particular. The trust reposed in the watchmen's such as renders him capable of great detriment to the community. He that undertakes in this work from secular motives will meet with disappointment. What a gross absurdity as this for a man to command religion to others while he is a stranger to himself! "The pious preacher will commend the saviour from the personal fund of his own experience." Being smitten with the love of Christ himself

with zeal and fervour will he speak of the divine glory! Love to Christ will tend to make a minister faithful and successful. The importance of this point urges me to be copious on the subject were it not too obvious to require a long discussion.

2. Wisdom and prudence are important qualifications in minsters: hence that injunction of the great preacher. Matt. x. 16. Be you therefore wise as serpents and harmless as doves. He is a man of spiritual understanding whose soul is irradiated with the beams of the Son of Righteousness,—has received an unction form the holy one,—is taught by the Word and Spirit, walks in the light of God's countenance. He has seen the deceit of his own heart,—knows the intrigues of the enemy,—sees the many snares to which the souls of men are exposed,—and not being ignorant of the devices of satan, he will endeavour to carry to spiritual campaign with that care and prudence that he shall not get advantage. He knows that he has a subtle enemy to oppose, and human nature, replete with enmity against the gospel; and will endeavour in every effort to conduct with that wisdom and circumspection as shall appear most likely to prove successful.

3. Patience is another qualification very necessary in a spiritual watchman. His breast being inspired with love to the cause, he will stand the storms of temptations; will not be disheartened by all the fatigues, and sufferings to which his work exposes him; but will endure hardness as a good soldier of Jesus Christ.

4. Courage and fortitude, must constitute a part of the character of a gospel minister. A sentinel who is worthy of that station, will not fear the formidable appearance of the enemy nor tremble at their menaces. None of these things remove him, neither will he count his life dear to him to defend a cause so very important. He has the spirit of the intrepid Nehemiah, "Should

such a man as I flee?" He stands fast in the face; quits himself like a man, and is strong.

5. Nor let us we forget to mention vigilance or close attention to the businesses signed him, as an essential qualification in a minister of Christ. A man does not answer the idea of a watchmen unless his mind is engaged in the business. The word, which we have rendered *watch*, in the text, signifies, in the original, too awake, and abstain from sleeping.[1] Indeed all the purposes of the watch set upon the wall are frustrated if he sleeps on guard; thereby himself and the whole army are liable to falling easy prey to the cruel depredations of the enemy. The spiritual watchmen is not to sleep, but to watch the first motion of the enemy and give the alarm; lest souls perish through his drowsiness and inattention.

III. To show, that ministers must give account to God of their conduct, more especially as it respects the people of their charge.

This solemn consideration as suggested in the text: 'Tis the design of preaching to make things ready for the Day of Judgment. 2 Cor. ii. 16. To the one we are the savour of death unto death; and to the other the savour of life unto life: We are fitting men for the Master's use—preparing affairs for that decisive court. This supposes that things must be laid open before the great assembly at the Day of Judgment; or, why is it that there are so many things that related thereto and our preferences therefor.

The work of a gospel minister has a peculiar relation to futurity: An approaching judgment is that too which every subject is pointing and which renders every sentiment to be inculcated, vastly solemn, and interesting. Ministers are accountable creatures in common with other men; and we have the unerring tes-

---
[1] Legh's *Critica Sacra*

timony of scripture, that God shall bring every work into judgment, with every secret thing, whether it be good or whether it be evil. Eccl. xii. 14. If there is none of our conduct too minute to be cognizable, we may well conclude that such important affairs that relate to the working office of gospel ministers will not pass unnoticed.

Arguments maybe taken from the names given to the ministers of Christ, that they must give account. They are *soldiers, ambassadors, servants, stewards, angels,* &c. Which points out the relation they and their work stands in to God: that they are sent of God and are amenable to him that sent them; as a servant or steward, is to give account to his Lord and Master, with respect to his faithfulness in the trust reposed in him. God tells Ezekiel, If watchmen are not faithful and souls perish through their neglect, then he will require their blood at the hands of such careless watchmen. It is evident that primitive ministers were influenced a faithfulness from a view of the solemn account they expected to give it the Day of Judgment. This gave rise to those words, Acts iv. 19, "But Peter and John answered and said onto them, whether it be right in the sight of God to harken onto you more then onto God, judge ye." If God's omniscience is emotive to faithfulness, it must be in this view that he will not let our conduct passed unnoticed, but call list to an account.

It was approaching judgment that engrossed the attention of St. Paul and made him exhort Timothy to study to approve himself onto God. This made the beloved disciple speak of having boldness in the Day of Judgment, 1 John iv. 17.

The divine glory is an object only worthy of attention; and to display his holy character, was the design of God in creation; as there was other beings existing antecedent thereto, to attract the mind of Jehovah; and we are sure that God is pursuing the same things still, and always will. He is in one mind and who can turn him? Job xxiii. 13. There is no conceivable object that bears any proportion with the glory of God; and for him ever to aim at anything else, would be incompatible with his perfections. The Day of Judgment is designed to be a comment on all other days; at which time God's government of the world, and their conduct towards him, will be publicly investigated, that the equity of divine administration may appear conspicuous before the assembled universe. It is called a day on which the Son of Man is *revealed*. Luke xvii. 30. The honour of God requires that matters be publicly and particularly attended two; that evidences are summoned at this open court: Hence the saints are to judge the world. 1 Cor. vi. 2.

It will conduce to the mutual happiness of faithful ministers and people, to have matter laid open before the bar of God, as in the words following our text, but they may do it with joy and not with grief. The apostle speaks of some ministers and people who should have reciprocal joy in the day of the Lord Jesus–which supposes that ministers and the people in their charge are to meet another day as having something special with each other. The connection between ministers and people is such, as renders them capable of saying much for, or against the people of their charge; and if hearers making the same observations with respect to their teachers; and in this way the mercy and justice of God will appear illustrious.

Since, therefore, the work of gospel ministers has such a new relation to a Judgment Day;—since they are accountable creatures, and their work so momentous;—since it is a sentiment that is had so powerful and influence all true ministers and all ages of the world: Also there connection is such as to render them capable of saying many things relating to the people of their charge. Above all, since it displays a divine glory are so highly concerned in this matter; we may without hesitation adopt the idea in the text, that ministers have a solemn account to give to their great Lord and Master how they discharge the trust reposed in them.

IV. We are to inquire what influence such considerations will have on the true ministers of Christ; or when they may be said to preach and act as those who must give account.

1. Who properly expect to give account, will be very careful to examine themselves with respect to the motives by which they are influenced to undertake this work. He will view himself acting in the presence of a heart-searching God, who requires truth in the inward parts, and will shortly call him to an account for all the exercises of his heart. He will search every corner of his soul, whether the divine honor, or something else, is the object of his pursuit. He has been taught, by the rectitude of divine law, that God will not pass by transgression, but will judge the secrets of men. The work will appear so great, that nature will recoil at the thought, like Jeremiah, "Ah, Lord God! behold, I cannot speak, for I am a child." Or with the great apostle, "Who is sufficient for these things?" The true disciple of Jesus will not thrust himself forward in the ministry, like a heedless usurper; but with the greatest caution and self-diffidence.

2. A faithful watchmen will manifest that he expects to give an account by being very careful to know his duty, and will take all proper ways which are in his power to become acquainted with it. He will study, as the apostle directs Timothy, to show himself approved unto God. He will give attention to reading, meditation, and prayer; will often call in divine aid, on account of his own insufficiency. As a faithful soldier will be careful to understand his duty; so the spiritual watchmen

would here closely to the word of God for his guide and directory.

3. A minister that watches for souls as one who expects to give an account, will have none to please but God. When he studies his sermons, this will not be his inquiry, "How shall I form my discourse so as to pleasing and gratify to humours of men and get their applause?" But, "How show I preach so is to do honour to God, and meet with the approbation of my judge?" This will be his daily request at the throne of grace. This will be ten thousand times better to him than the vain flattery of men. His discourses will not be circulated to gratify the carnal heart, but he will not shun to declare the whole counsel of God.

The solemn account that the minister expects to give on another day will direct him in the choice of this subject; he would dwell upon those things which have more direct relation to the eternal world. He will not entertain his audience with empty speculations or vain philosophy; but with things that concern their everlasting welfare. Jesus Christ and him crucified will be the great topic and darling theme of his preaching. If he needs to save souls, like a skilful physician, he will endeavour to lead his patients into a view of their maladies and then point them to a bleeding Saviour as the only way of recovery. The faithful watchmen will give the alarm at the approach of the enemy, and will blow the trumpet in the ears of the sleeping sinner and endeavour to awaken him.

4. The pious preacher will endeavour to adapt is discourses to the understanding of his hearers. "He will not be ambitious of saying fine things to win applause, but of saying useful things to win souls." He will consider that he has the weak as well as the strong, children as well as adults to speak to, and that he must be accountable for the blood of their souls if they perish through his neglect. This will influence him to study

plainness more than politeness; also he will labour to accommodate his sermons to the different states or circumstances of his hearers; he will have comforting and encouraging lessons to see before the children of God; while the terrors of the law are to be proclaimed in the ears of the impenitent. He will strive to preach distinguishing that every hearer may have his portion.--The awful scenes of approaching judgment, will have an influence upon the Christian preacher with respect to the *manner* in which he will deliver himself. He will guard against that low and vulgar style that tends to degrade religion; but his language will in some measure correspond with those very solemn and affecting things that do engage his heart and tongue. He will not substitute a whining tone in the room of the sermon; which, to speak no worse of it, is a sort of satire upon the gospel, tending greatly to deprecate it solemnity and importance, and to bring it into contempt; but the judgment will appear so awful and his attention so captivated with it, that his accents will be the result of a mind honestly and engagingly taking up with a subject vastly important. "Such a preacher will not come into the pulpit as an actor comes upon the stage, to personate a feigned character and forget his real one; to sentiments or represent passion to his own."[2] It is not to display his talents, but like one who feels the weight of eternal things, he will not address his hearers as though judgment was a mere empty sound; but viewing eternity just before them, any congregation up on the frontiers of it, this whole eternal state depends upon a few uncertain moments; Oh! with what zeal and fervour will he speak! How will death, judgment, and eternity appear as it were in every feature and every word! Out of the abundance of his heart his mouth will speak. His hearers will easily perceive but the preacher is one who expects to give account. He will study and preach

---

2 Fordyce

with reference to a judgment to come, and deliver every sermon in some respect as if it were his last, not knowing when his Lord will call him or his hearers to account. We are not to suppose that his zeal will vent itself and the frightful bellowings of enthusiasm; but he will speak forth the words of truth in soberness, with modesty, and with Christian decency.

5. Those who watch for souls as those who expect to give an account, will endeavour to know as much as may be the state of the souls committed to their charge, that they may be in a better capacity to do them good. They will point out those errors and dangers which they may see approaching; and when they see souls taken by the enemy, they will exert themselves to deliver them from the snare of the devil. The onward department of the faithful minister will correspond with his preaching: he will reprove, rebuke, warning his people from house to house. The weighty affairs of another world will direct his daily walk and conversation and and all places and on every occasion.

A Few Particular Addresses

First, to him who is about to set apart to the work of gospel ministry in this place.

Dear Sir,

From the preceding observations, you will easily see that the work before you is great and solemn; and I hope this is a lesson you have been taught otherwise; the former acquaintance I have had with you gives me reason to hope that this is the case. You are about to have these souls committed to your care; you are to be placed as a watchman upon the walls of this part of Zion. I doubt not but that it is with trembling you enter upon this work. The relation that this day's business has with a judgment to come renders the scene affecting. Your mind I trust has already anticipated the solemn moment when you must meet these people before the bar of God. The good profession you are this state to make is before many witnesses; saints and wicked men are beholding; the angels are looking down upon us; above all the great God with complacency or disapprobation beholds the transactions of this day; he sees what motives govern you, and he will proclaim it before the assembled universe. Oh! solemn and affecting thought! The work before you is great and requires great searching of heart, great self-diffidence, and self abasement. How necessary that you feel your dependence upon God; you cannot perform any part of your work without his help; under a sense of your weakness, repair to him for help. Would you be a successful minister, you must be a praying dependent one; do all in the name and strength of the Lord Jesus. Would you be faithful in watching for the souls of men, you must be much and watching your own heart. If you are careless with respect to your own soul, you will be also with respect to others. Although the work is too great for you, yet let such considerations as these revive your desponding heart. That the cause is good, better than life, you may well give up all for it. 'Tis the cause of God, and that which will prove victorious in spite of all opposition from men or devils–that God has promised to be with his ministers to the end of the world–that the work is delightful. Paul somewhere blesses God for putting him into the work of the ministry –the campaign is short, your warfare will soon be accomplished–that the reward is great, being found faithful, you will receive a crown of glory that fadeth not away.

Secondly, we have a word to the church and congregation in this place.

My Brethren and Friends,

The importance of the work of a gospel minister suggests the weighty concerns of your souls. As ministers must give account how they preach and behave;

so hearers also are to be examined how they hear and improve. You are to hear with the view to the day of judgment, always remembering that there is no sermon or opportunity that you have in this life to repair for another world that shall go unnoticed at that decisive court. Your present exercises with respect to the solemn affairs of this day will then come up to public view.

God we trust is this day sending one to watch for your souls: should not this excite sentiments of gratitude in your breasts? Shall God makes so much care for your souls and you neglect them? How unreasonable will it be for you to despise the pious instruction of your watchmen? You will herein wrong your own souls and it will be an evidence that you love death. You will bear with him in not accommodating his sermons to your vitiated tastes because *he must give account*. His work is great and you must pray for him; as in the verse following the text the apostle says, "Brethren pray for us." Is it the business of your minister to watch for your souls with such indefatigable assiduity, you easily see how necessary it is that you do what you can to strengthen him in this work. That you minister to his temporal wants, that he may give himself wholly to these things. The great backwardness among people in general with respect to this matter at present is an unfavorable aspect. "Who goeth to warfare anytime at his own charges? Who planteth a vineyard and eateth not of the fruit thereof? or feedeth a flock and earth not of the milk of the flock?" 1 Cor. ix. 7.

Doubtless this man is sent here for the rise and fall of many in this place. We hope we will be used as a means of leading some to Christ; while on the other hand, we even tremble at the thought, he may fit others for more aggravated condemnation. Take heed how you hear.

A few words to the assembly in general to close the subject.

What has been said about the character and work of gospel ministers shows us at once it is a matter in which we are all deeply interested. The greater part of the people present, I expect to see you no more until I meet them at that day, which has been the main subject of the foregoing discourse. With respect to the character of the people present, we can say little about them; only this we may observe, *they are all dying creatures*, hastening to the grave and to judgment. There must we meet you–there an account of this day's work will come up to view–there each one must give an account concerning the right discharge of the work assigned him. The preacher must give an account, and you that hear also. Let me say to such as our yet in their sins and proclaim it from this part of the wall of Zion, that the enemy of your souls is at hand–that destruction awaits you. Oh! flee! flee! to Christ Jesus; bow to his sovereignty; know this, but except you were born again and become new creatures in the dispositions of your mind, you cannot be saved. Shall ministers watch and pray for your souls night and day and you pay no attention to them? Since they are so valuable, having such a relation to God, did men regard divine glory they would regard their souls as being designed to exhibit it.

Be instructed then, to delay no longer, but by repentance toward God and faith in the Lord Jesus Christ make peace with him before you were summoned before his awful bar. Let me bear testimony against your practice too common on such occasions as this: Many people think it is time for carnal mirth and dissipation, that which nothing can be more provoking to God nor incommensurate with that day and strict account that such an occasion tends to exciting the mind. May all, both ministers and people, be exhorted to diligence in their work, that finally we me adopt the language of the blessed Apostle, "As also ye have acknowledged us in part that we are your rejoicing, even as ye also are ours in the day of the Lord Jesus."

Amen

Sermon II.

THE IMPORTANT CONCERNS OF MINISTERS, AND THE PEOPLE OF THEIR CHARGE, AT THE DAY OF JUDGMENT

A SERMON DELIVERED AT RUTLAND, ORANGE SOCIETY
APRIL 22D, 1797
AT THE INTERNMENT OF THE REV. ABRAHAM CARPENTER,
THEIR WORTHY PASTOR

For what is our hope, or joy, or crown of rejoicing? Are not even ye in the presence of the Lord Jesus Christ at his coming?
1 Thessalonians ii. 19.

The second coming of Christ is a source of peculiar joy and consolation to the people of God; it is a day in which their hopes and expectations will be fully answered. Tribulation attends the good man while in this life; the scenes of divine Providence are mysterious, and many things unaccountable and insignificant without a day of judgment; they will then be explained and adjusted, to the joy and admiration of all who love

Christ's appearing. Many of the events that take place in this life stand in a solemn relation to the judgment day, and none more so than the gospel ministry; hence it is that the attention of the true servants of Christ is so much taken up with a future state. St. Paul, being detained from the church of Thessalonica, sends this epistle as a token of his love and respect to them; in which he anticipates that blessed period when he should meet them at the bar of Christ, which would afford such joy and satisfaction as to more than compensate for all their sorrow, more especially for his being prevented a personal interview with those to whom he wrote. *"For what is our hope, or joy, or crown of rejoicing? Are not even ye in the presence of our Lord Jesus Christ at his coming?"* We have two very important ideas suggested in the words. One is, that ministers and their people must meet each other at the day of judgment. The second is, that although ministers are often separated from their hearers in this life, yet the people of God among whom a pious preacher finishes his work will be a cause or crown of peculiar joy and satisfaction at the second coming of Christ.

With respect to the first point, we may observe, to give us a striking contrast between this and the coming world, we are in the present state subject to many vicissitudes.

What changes are taking place in empires, states, societies, and families! In nothing is this more observable than in matters relating to ministers and the people of their charge. A persecuting spirit, that prevailed in the apostolic age, was often a means of parting friends, and especially of driving preachers from churches. The same cause has had influence in every age of the church; but if religious societies are so happy as to escape such a calamity, yet it pleases the Great Head of the church, in his sovereign wisdom, to separate ministers and their people by death; this gives feeling to a pious preacher, and in some degree has influence in every sermon he delivers. That all mankind will be collected before the bar of Christ, to see the great and intricate affairs of the universe adjusted, is a plain dictate of reason and Scripture; but that many will meet there as having mutual concerns with each other, is evident. More especially ministers and the people once committed to their charge doubtless will appear in some sense as distinct societies, as having particular and personal matters to attend to. This supposes that they will have a knowledge of each other; for without this, the purposes of their meeting in such a manner could not be answered. How far this will extend, or by what means it will be conveyed, is too curious to inquire. It seems, unless we are able by some means to distinguish those from others with whom we have been intimate in this life, the designs of a future judgment will in some measure be frustrated. The great end of that day is to illustrate divine truth, or make that appear conspicuous to created intelligence. To effect this, God will make use of mankind as instruments; this is the method he takes in this life, and doubtless it will be most eligible in the world to come. For our acquaintance to be summoned as witnesses for or against us at this court, will perhaps be the best means to administer conviction. In this way the great God can speak in language easy for finite creatures to understand. One design of the world being divided into distinct societies and communities, is doubtless to prepare matters for the day of judgment. The relation between ministers and people is such as renders them capable of saying much about each other; in this way the justice and mercy of God will be illustrated, Divine proceedings vindicated, and every mouth stopped. It is our conduct in this life that will direct Divine proceeding towards us at the final judgment; that the equity of God's administrations may appear, 'tis necessary that our characters be clearly investigated. The salvation and damnation of many souls will be through the instrumentality of faithful and unfaithful watchmen; this is an idea contained in the charge God gave to Ezekiel, 32d chapter. It will be necessary that the motives by which ministers have been influenced in their work be brought out to view; for without sincerity of heart they can never execute their office with any degree of true faithfulness, and are a high affront to God, and a vile imposition on the people.

At the day of judgment the *doctrines* with which a minister has entertained his hearers must be examined. However doctrinal preaching may be discarded by many, and such words as *metaphysical, abstruse,* &c., are often made use of to obstruct free and candid inquiry; yet it is evident that one great end of the gospel ministry is to disseminate right sentiments; hence it is that Paul so often exhorts Timothy to take heed to his *doctrine*. Sound doctrine, as well as good practice, is necessary to constitute the Christian character: "Who soever transgresseth, and abideth not in the *doctrine* of Christ, hath not God." 2 John, 9.

A careful inquiry will be made whether an empty parade of learning, elegance of style, &c., have been the main things with which a people have been entertained, tending only to gratify vain curiosity, and to fix the attention of the hearers on the speaker. This made St. Paul contemn such a mode of preaching, and determine not to know anything save Jesus Christ, and him crucified, 1 Cor. ii. 2. Whether vague, equivocal expressions have been used to convey, or rather to obscure the truths of the gospel, by which anything and almost everything may be understood. This is causing the trumpet to give an uncertain sound, and has no tendency to impress or give feeling to the mind, as is the case with the words of the wise, being as *goads* and *nails,* Eccle. xii. 11. Whether to please men has had greater influence in our composing and delivering our sermons than the glory of God and the good of souls. People will be examined at the bar of Christ whether they have not been dealt plainly with; been told their characters and danger; that they are wholly opposed to God, destitute of everything that is holy or morally good; that they are by nature under the curse of God's law, exposed every moment to endless woe; that they are hopeless and helpless in themselves; the necessity of the renewing influences of the spirit; the nature of their impotence, that it consists in an evil heart; that therefore they are altogether inexcusable; and are criminal in proportion to the degree of their inability; that nothing short of repentance towards God and faith in the Lord Jesus Christ is the immediate duty of all that hear the gospel.

Ministers and their people must meet before the judgment-seat of Christ, to give an account whether the true character of God has in any good measure been investigated; as a sin-hating and sin-revenging God.

Without this the character of God is kept out of sight, people left in the dark, and are not able to determine whether they love or hate the true God.

It must be known whether people have had the character and work of the Redeemer set before them; the design of his sufferings, the efficacy of his blood, and the necessity of our union to him. The manner in which divine truth has been delivered will be a matter worthy of serious examination at that day; whether with that earnestness and fervour becoming the vast importance and solemnity of gospel truth, tending to affect the mind. The deportment or examples of ministers among their people will be closely attended to; their private visits, exhortations, and reproofs, holy desires and wrestlings for the souls of their hearers, will not escape public notice; the improvement that people have made of such advantages will be brought into public view.

How often people have attended on the ministration of the word, and the manner how, will be matters of serious concern at the judgment day. Those excuses that men make for neglecting public worship will be weighed in a just scale. Whether people have so far contributed to the temporal support of their ministers as to enable them to devote themselves to the service of Christ; or, by too great neglect, have not obstructed the gospel, robbed God, wounded their own souls.

It will be useful that the *time* of a minister's continuance among a people be known, as it will serve to set be characters of gospel despisers in a true point of light. That ministers and the people of their charge will meet each other at the bar of Christ, is suggested in my text, and in other parts of the sacred writings. It has already been observed that in this way truth will appear conspicuous, and the conduct of God will be indicated, and the designs of a judgment day in the best manner answered. It may further be observed, that the matters relating to the gospel ministry are of such magnitude that it appears important that they be attended to; they concern a judgment day and an eternal state. When ministers and people meet in the house of God, it is an acknowledgment that they believe in a future state of retribution, and is a sort of appeal to the day of judgment. The influence of a faithful or unfaithful minister is such as to affect unborn ages; it will commonly determine the sentiments and characters of their successors, and in this way they may be doing good or evil after they are dead, and even to the second coming of Christ. That God's hatred towards false teachers, and against those who choose them, together with their criminality, may appear, it will be necessary that these matters be laid open at the tribunal of Christ. As a proof of the matter under consideration, I may only add, that there always has been an important controversy, in a greater or less degree, between ministers and part of their people; it is so with faithful preachers and some of their hearers; wicked men oppose the doctrines they preach, and will not be convinced. Unfaithful preachers have advocates and opposers; the dispute involved the character of Christ; it cannot be settled in this world. How necessary that ministers and people meet at the great day, to have the matter decided, the doctrines of Christ vindicated, and the characters of ministers or people exonerated.

II. Another important idea contained in the text is, that the church or people of God among whom a faithful minister finishes his work, will be a cause or crown of peculiar joy or rejoicing at the coming of Christ. It will be matter of great satisfaction to sit down with Abraham, Isaac, and Jacob, and other saints at that day; but the Scriptures represent that godly ministers will derive peculiar joy from the pious part of their congregations, Dan. xii. 3; 2 Cor. i. 14; Phil. ii. 16. Reflecting on past providences will be a source of great joy at the day of judgment; and as many things have taken place between a minister and his people in which they are more particularly conversant and interested, when they come to be explained it will afford special joy and admiration; as they have been companions in tribulations, so now it is likely they will be in a more peculiar sense co-partners in joy, and help each other in magnifying the Lord for special favours, and displays of divine power and grace on their behalf.

The prayers and struggles of pious teachers have been for Zion in general, and for those over whom the Holy Ghost has made them overseers in particular. Now God will give their hearers who have been converted through their instrumentality as a kind of reward and fruit of their travail or labour. When it appears that God has made use of the true ministers of Christ for the conversion of some of the souls once committed to heir charge, it will excite wonder, joy, and humility in the minds of pious teachers, that God should deign to honour them as instruments of such glorious work, by which they will be led to adore sovereign grace and condescending love. As it is often through the painful labours of Christ's servants that souls are brought home to God, doubtless he will approve of such virtues by conferring signal honours on those who have turned many to righteousness, who will shine as stars forever and ever.

Pious people will give such account of their faithful teachers as will meet with the approbation of God, which will be expressed by that heavenly plaudit, "Well done, good and faithful servant!" Their mutual accounts will be given up with joy, and not with grief, Hebrews xiii. 17. The hopes and expectations of such ministers are great, as the apostle suggests in the text– For what is our hope, or joy, or crown of rejoicing? are not even ye? &c. He speaks of it as the earnest hope and expectation of all Christ's ministers, by calling it our hope. They reflect with pleasure on the approaching happy moment, and when it comes it will greatly gratify their holy desires.

That it will be possible to hold equal communion with all the saints, especially at one time, in the invisible world, perhaps is not admissible. It appears that the wicked who have been associates in sin here will be companions of torments hereafter, Luke xvi. 28.

They are to be gathered like the standing corn, and to be bound in *bundles* to burn. It is more than possible that the righteous who have lived together in this life, will have a more intimate access to each other in the world to come.

If it will be useful for them to meet in some sense as distinct societies, perhaps it will subserve the interest of the universe that they in a degree continue so. It is the character of the true church of Christ that they treat his ministers with respect in this life, accounting them as the ministers of Christ and stewards of the mysteries of God, 1 Cor. iv. 1. They help them in their work, 2 Cor. i. 11. God will in the great day reward people for such kindness; as hereby they express their love to Christ, Matt. xxv. 40. This will gratify the benevolent feelings of Christ's servants; at the same time fill them with holy admiration and deep humility, that what has been done to such poor sinful creatures should be taken notice of.

Ministers and the people of their charge will assist each other, and be united in bringing a verdict against the wicked and impenitent among whom they lived while on earth. The saints are to judge the world, 1 Cor. vi. 2. One way by which they will do this will doubtless be to declare before angels and men what they know about them, or their conduct in this life. An attachment to divine justice will make this delightful work. Ministers must declare what and how they have preached to them, and the bad improvement they have made of the gospel, so far as it has come under their observation; how they have despised and mocked the messengers of the Lord, contemned his word and ordinances. Pious hearers can witness to the same things, and in this way the mutual testimony of godly ministers and people will be strengthened and supported, and Divine proceedings against impenitent sinners vindicated. Thus the church will be a crown of joy to her faithful pastor.

IMPROVEMENT

I. We may infer from this subject that the gospel ministry is of God, and that we ought to seek its welfare, and use suitable exertions for its support.

Doth Scripture and reason dictate that it is of so much importance, especially as it relates to a judgment day, we may conclude that God would not do without it, and we may see Divine wisdom and goodness in the institution. Nothing more conducive of Divine glory, and salutary to men, than the preaching of the gospel.

Without these glad tidings are proclaimed, the incarnation of Christ is vain. Nothing but opposition to God, and disregard to his glory, will make men indifferent to the preaching of the gospel. A rejection of Christ and his ministers has commonly vice and open profanity for its inseparable companions. The opposition that the impenitent part of mankind have made to the servants of Christ, has doubtless in some measure had its rise from a consciousness that they must meet them at the bar of Christ, to their disadvantage.

We may conclude, that, since the gospel ministry is so very useful, it will be continued to the end of the world.

2. When a faithful minister is taken away, it ought seriously to be regarded. But few ways perhaps that God shows greater displeasure against a people than in calling his ambassadors home. By this he threatens to put an end to his treaty of peace, and become irreconcilable. It may sometimes be the case that God has no more chosen or elect ones among them. When Paul and Barnabas were preaching at Antioch, as many as were *ordained* to eternal life believed, then they departed, Acts xiii. All the encouragement for a minister to preach among a people, so far as the salvation of souls ought to be a motive, is the doctrine of election. After the death of a faithful minister there is less hope of a people.

We may further observe, when it is considered that we are to meet them no more in the house of God, to hear them declare unto us the words of reconciliation; but our next interview will be at the tribunal of Christ, to hear them testify for or against us, how affecting the consideration! It is more solemn to die than if we had never been favoured with the gospel ministry. People, whether they hear or forbear, shall know, to their joy or sorrow, that there hath been a prophet among them, Ezek. ii. 5.

3. The subject affords direction how ministers should preach, and how a people ought to hear, viz., with death and judgment in view. It is this that makes preaching and hearing a serious matter, and renders the house of God so very solemn. We must soon meet before the bar of Christ, and perhaps before the next Sabbath, to have our sermons and our hearing ex amined by Him who is infinite in knowledge, and is present in every congregation. Did we always consider these things, it would tend to abolish that coldness, drowsiness, and indifference, that too often attend the ministers of the gospel, and that formal spirit which is too apparent among hearers. How would it check that levity of mind and disorderly behaviour that presumptuous creatures often indulge in the house of God. *How dreadful is this place!* — is a reflection suitable on all occasions, and more especially when we meet for public devotion.

4. The surviving widow and children will for a moment suffer the word of exhortation. Are not you in some sense his hope and joy? Was it not a reflection that tended to smooth the rugged road through death, that he should meet you before the bar of Christ, and that you would be a crown of rejoicing in that day? If ministers and people are to meet each other before the tribunal of Christ, as having special business together, then we may conclude that this will be the case with particular families, such as husbands and wives, parents and children; you can say much about each other upon that occasion, having for so long a time composed one family on earth.

You, who are this day called to mourn, must give an account how you have improved his public and more private admonitions; and especially this providence. The present occasion, however solemn, will appear more so at the great day. Consider, that although he is gone to return no more, yet God, the source of consolation, ever lives. His promises are always new to the widow and fatherless. That God who gave has taken him away. But still he lives in another state, and is more useful to the universe than he could be in this world. God's people always die in the best time, manner, and place. You have only time to take up the body and bury it, set your houses in order, and follow him. Manifest your love to the deceased by preparing to meet him, and make his heart glad in the day of the Lord Jesus. Contemplate the rectitude of divine government, and a future world, and be still.

Let the children remember, that to have a pious faithful parent taken away is an unspeakable loss. Your father has done much for your bodies, but we trust more for your souls; never, never forget his prayers and admonitions. Can you, dare you meet him at the bar of Christ in impenitence? Should this be the case, instead of those endearing and parental caresses that you have received from him in this life, he will join with the Judge of all in saying, *Depart*! He will declare what he has done for you, and condemn you. Let your mother experience that tender regard and kind assistance, during her short continuance with you, as becomes dutiful, obedient children. Make her heart glad by a holy life, and let your father live daily before her eyes in your pious examples.

Let me say a word to the church and congregation this place. Dear friends, I am not a stranger to those mournful sensations that the present melancholy providence tends to inspire. I trust I am a hearty mourner with you, and am a sharer in your loss.

By the foregoing observations you have reason to conclude that you have lost a faithful minister.

You can't forget those solemn and affectionate warnings that he has given you from the desk, nor those pious examples he has set before you. He has preached his last sermon. Your next meeting must be before the tribunal of Christ, where those sermons you have heard him deliver in this life will come to view, and the improvement you have made of them. Will you, brethren, be his crown of rejoicing in that day? If you were his hope and joy in this life, you doubtless are still. It is with satisfaction we trust that he this moment looks forward to that day, when he expects to see this the dear people once committed to his charge; and doubtless he hopes to meet some of you as crowns of rejoicing. Oh! do not disappoint the hope and expectations of your reverend pastor. Manifest your love to him by imitating his holy examples, and by having those heavenly instructions that he so often inculcated always in remembrance; and by preparing to give him joy in the day of the Lord Jesus. Examine what improvement you have made of the gospel ministry while you had it; and whether too great inattention has not had influence in its being removed. Have you ever experienced the power and efficacy of the gospel upon your own souls? Have you by the Holy Spirit been formed into the moral likeness of the blessed God, and into the image of his son Jesus? Or have you been contented with the mere form of godliness? Have you not, through sloth and unbelief, neglected attending on the preaching of the gospel during the residence of your pastor among you? Oh! what account will such gospel despisers have to give another day! Consider, I entreat you, how dreadful it will be to have these things brought into view when you come to meet your minister, who was once, and perhaps is now, an eyewitness of your conduct, and will testify against you to your everlasting condemnation!

Your minister, though dead, now speaketh. He preaches a most solemn lecture to us all this day on mortality.

You will, as it were, hear his voice when you look on the place of public worship, where he and you so often attended—when you look on his grave, which is here among you—and when you look to the second coming of Christ. Think often of that day. Let the Sabbath, and worship of God, be still dear unto you; and remember him who has spoken unto you the word of God, whose faith follow.

www.ingramcontent.com/pod-product-compliance
Lightning Source LLC
Chambersburg PA
CBHW010004110526
44587CB00024BA/4019